Breast Cancer:
A Poem in Five Acts

poems by

Kari Wergeland

Finishing Line Press
Georgetown, Kentucky

Breast Cancer:
A Poem in Five Acts

Copyright © 2018 by Kari Wergeland
ISBN 978-1-63534-570-4 First Edition
All rights reserved under International and Pan-American Copyright Conventions.
No part of this book may be reproduced in any manner whatsoever without written permission from the publisher, except in the case of brief quotations embodied in critical articles and reviews.

Publisher: Leah Maines
Editor: Christen Kincaid
Cover Art: Pam Kersey
Author Photo: Ian Cummings Photography
Cover Design: Elizabeth Maines McCleavy

Printed in the USA on acid-free paper.
Order online: www.finishinglinepress.com
        also available on amazon.com

                Author inquiries and mail orders:
                      Finishing Line Press
                      P. O. Box 1626
                  Georgetown, Kentucky 40324
                          U. S. A.

Table of Contents

Act One
Diagnosis 1

Act Two
Surgery 5

Act Three
Chemo 10

Act Four
Radiation 20

Act Five
Follow-up 30

Special thanks to Moores Cancer Center at UC San Diego Health and all the helpful people I encountered while undergoing breast cancer treatment, including the physicians who guided me through the three trials:

> *Dr. Sarah Blair*
> *Dr. Teresa Helsten*
> *Dr. Catheryn Yashar*

ACT ONE: Diagnosis

What appears
to be vibrant health this winter
has a flaw,
cells mutating
into a suspicious mass—
four centimeters by one—
not striking any nerve
to announce its place in the body;
though once I was told it was there,
but did not know
the extent of its nature,
I dreamed of a sixteen-legged creature—
each long appendage a pointy thing
stabbing flesh,
digging in to hold on tight.
I was sure it was a killer.

This pink ribbon is an archetype:
the whole story,
a modern fairytale,
where there's a maze
filled with technological wonders,
where the exit is not clear.

The biopsy
was so expertly done,
I could not feel the needle.

I do feel craziness.
Fear.

Am I beginning a war
with cells,
cells I can't see,

a war
that will grip
as I battle back
and back?

Some brush this off,
"Oh, you'll get through it,"
but a mass seated inside strength,
endurance,
releasing seeds of menace—
is a sinkhole.

For if breast cancer appears
in one in eight women,
I must have 64 sisters.
I count half that.

Escape.

I move into the urban fray
on a nightwalk with a friend.
When we cross the busy street,
I glance up to note huge neon letters,
bright, bright pink
against a black, black sky—
the BOULEVARD.

They're classifying genes,
mapping families,
trying to predict things
like factors that increase
breast cancer risk,
which could mean
a double mastectomy
or an annual MRI.

Consideration:

Let me die in my sleep
or of a heart attack,
not some drawn-out struggle
that takes up people's time.

An MRI is ordered
for activity not seen
on mammograms,
the ultrasound screen.

The results dawdle
as cancer pops out at me
on billboards, TV, magazines—

Some good news:

No mutations detected
in the seventeen genes
that might predict things;
and only one tumor
thrives
in my left breast.

I can keep them—
for now.

They do plan
to remove this mass,
the sentinel lymph node
(perhaps add chemo infusions);
radiate trouble spots;
prescribe a hormone blocker;

so I can walk away free—
nothing overly different
except scars on my chest,
side effects,
and a mind that has aged
in a way that can't be marked
the way rings score a tree.

And still the sixteen-legged thing
tries to hide.

Blue-green dye
should reveal its reach.

ACT TWO: Surgery

Pre-op chaotic—
I'm in a brittle drum,
though my vitals deliver
excellent blood pressure,
one-hundred-percent lung function,
calm pulse;
seem immune
to the sixteen-legged thing
not pinching any nerve
destined to be blocked
before the surgeon
draws a margin
to remove this threat.

I've got a little cell
where it's easier to doze
after they attach a blower
to my inflatable hospital gown
and warm air puffs around me.

Delay—
descent into the long hours.

It's even easier to relax
when they shoot painkillers into my blood,
numbing all the nerves
on the left side of my chest.

Though I'm already drugged,
I force myself to pay attention
to the operating room—
the big round lamps,
the narrow bed.

How are you feeling?

I don't hear this question.
I wake and speak at once.
"I'm nauseated."
When I say these words a second time,
a nurse reaches for a barf bag
and I throw up the nothing
I have eaten all day.

My urine is a spectacular blue-green.

On the ride home,
I find myself marveling,
I still have breasts!

Life feels bandaged,
suspended swing,
pause before the results come in.
Doves in the neighborhood sing.
I'm the one in a cage.
Outside,
fertility looms.

A walk on pavement
through Mission Trails Regional Park
seems safe from any fall
that might endanger my wounds,
till I look down to spot movement
in parallel motion with me.
I step back to study this snake,
four long feet of brownish-green
analog curves of power
with a rattler angling at forty-five degrees.
The reptile undulates south
on this cheerful day before spring.

Something needs to go
besides tumor and lymph nodes.
I've burrowed into an old burb.
Maybe it's me.

I rise to the occasion,
reach for optimism,
and I do find moments of mirth
(when a wild rabbit visits
to nibble my garden,
I invite the whole family)
but an underlying sense of unease
— dis—ease —
rides beneath my skin like a sliver,
like the port they might put in.

Wearing sexy green
for Saint Patrick's Day
after pulling the tape off
to note
they won't look weird
once the incision heals—
as long as radiation
doesn't change the wounded one.

A male lizard does push-ups
near the swimming pool
to impress a female
hanging over the edge of the patio.
She doesn't watch for long.
When he moves closer,
she darts into desert lilac.

I arrive at a fine old mansion
to sit in silence.
The sangha proceeds to set things up,
black cushions and zabutons.

I can't really help—
I have a broken wing.
I settle into a window seat,
watch birds flirting with their striped tails.
My eye catches smaller vibrations.
Closer inspection reveals a spider
moving in on a fly
stuck in filaments,
tough to see.
The spider injects venom into its catch.
The fly flashes its gauzy wings.
It looks like they are making love.
The spider rises above the fly,
leaving it to dangle beneath her.
Tied together,
they shoot up
and out of sight.

In the zendo
I learn I am one condition
affecting everything else,
the conditions I cannot control—

positive lymph nodes.

Another condition:

Ride to the underworld,
fueled by poison.

A dream surfaces—
small spider,
not so cruel, small;
and the sharply-pointed sixteen-legged thing
is no longer digging in.
The creature appears flattened,
like a child's penciled sun.

They call it mop-up,
one cancer survivor says—
what they do
when the path reveals clear margins.

ACT THREE: Chemo

The underworld can be reached
through two different ports.
Both will remove my hair,
turn me into a finicky eater—
put me at risk for infection.
One course leaves me below
one month longer,
requires surgery for a catheter
to protect my veins from burns—
twice as many infusions.
It could trigger what killed my father—leukemia.
A pedestrian IV could suffice
for the other.
But what if the other isn't enough?

Funny logic:
that which kept me youthful—
estrogen—
is now killing me.
And anyway,
instant menopause could be induced
in Hades.

You just turned 54.

Hades rhymes with ladies.

Waiting (for Hades)
for blood counts,
with a fresh IV neatly taped to one arm,
I notice the heads
that still have hair
expecting to be called—
young ones looking too healthy
to be there,
old ones like driftwood.

A recliner.
When a beep goes off,
the nurse asks for my name and birth date (again)
and switches the bag above my head.

Taxotere/Cytoxan
taking my life down
where I'll mourn what's been abandoned—
job interviews (plans for a new life),
a trek in the Grand Canyon of the Tuolumne,
fertility,
and voice lessons.

Occasionally a cheer can be heard.
For someone else,
infusions are through.

Bad night—
all those drugs tweaking me;
fatigue, even after sleeping.
I'm sleeping.
But when I can't sleep,
I'm on the brink of bone pain.

I move amongst the healthy
with an alien look,
feel their lives sprouting forward,
while mine remains buried
with my hair.

The nadir—
counts are low.
I consume more hand sanitizer,
avoid raw vegetables.

There are moments underground
when dark timbres darken even more,

and the mind curls around the sound
of "no way out,"
the way it feels
when those words are allowed to rise.

Midway through the first cycle,
I begin climbing back to Earth
to garden.

The second cycle
feels less gruesome to start,
though any little thing—
tingling in my fingers—
magnifies newfound vulnerability.

Not ready for breast cancer support,
hearing from women
who have endured thirty rounds of chemo
or are recovering
from a bilateral mastectomy or
their third scuffle with aberrant cells.

I am supported by people
who call, email, text,
send cards and gifts,
share movies, meals—
attend appointments with me.

Time crawls to the third cycle.

What seemed unsolvable before,
must be handed a ticket,
removed from the sickbay,
though it gnaws and whines and howls.
If only some adjuvant therapy
could sink it to dissolution.

In the end,
when you're down here
and it's nauseating,
no one can help.
Each black moment creeps by.

Namaste to gentle yoga!

Heading to the beach with those called
to keep me out of the pits.
We gaze at homes
where Sleeping Beauty might live—
old world elegance behind vines,
well-established trees,
and blooms in many colors.

In fairy tales,
everything comes in threes.
Like the three trials—
surgery, chemo, radiation—
that magic number three.
This is the end of week three
(chemo cycle two).
I'm stronger than week one,
though the poison has not completely left my pores.
In two days they'll give me more,
and the beach won't please me.
For now, I'm free
to walk toward the sea
beneath fecund jacarandas
littering the ground
with their lavender blossoms.
I want to veer toward Hotel Del,
sip on something out front
and watch the world pass.
When we get there,
this hunger has left me.

On the first day of cycle three,
I tramp up the steps to Earth
and bang on the gate
to what I would have done;
but today's blood draw
reveals a stressed-out liver,
one number too high.
Though I cling to the knob,
I'm sent back chemo-less
(stuck with more time).
Their elastic calendar
no longer fits with mine.

If only diarrhea
could purge what's left of these terrible cells
instead of slamming remnants of wellness
getting me through.
I want to STOP
this archaic therapy
that can't be healing
a thing.
But the shit just keeps coming
for twelve long hours,
even when it seems
no more
could possibly be wrung
from these bowels.

On Crystal Pier, the view
doubles back to life on Earth,
the backs of surfers riding in to shore.
When I turn my back on all of this,
stretch my thoughts
to the vastness before me,
a dolphin bursts into the air,
and for a moment appears
to dance on the waves
as its nose taps the sky.

No appetite for anything
but lying in the sand,
listening to the sea.

The third infusion sparks
my first hot flashes,
that promised menopause.
I arrive home to find a rattlesnake at my door.
This tells me what?
Something about sexuality?
Risk? Healing?
Shedding my skin?
It has just killed a lizard.

Some days are slow and gray,
the week called chemo brain.
And these chemicals smell
like toxic fumes—
explosions on the news,
everything poisoned.

Stretch before the home stretch.

I drive to yoga
inside a bubble
that skims Adams Avenue,
my old life forgotten.
When I do remember
some camping trip,
it comes up on a postcard.
I put it on the fridge.

According to my latest dream,
the little spider is dead.
I don't know
about the flattened
sixteen-legged thing.

Maybe it's strung a web
in one corner
of this underground den
to eye another.
Maybe it has vanished.

A thin sheet.
Add a blanket.
Back to the thin sheet.
Rhythm of underworld heat.

Time crawls and glides.

Some days I am free
to walk past a parked car
and note the open window,
the woman inside listening
to the professionally produced words drifting
toward me:

Success is getting what you want.
Happiness is loving what you get.

Four more weeks.

Another dream.
Another damned spider!
It skitters across the laminate floor.
Is this something chemo hasn't gotten?
Will radiation nail that sucker?

In an underworld mall,
I grab a table and wait
for a mechanic to service the car
I hope to use for my getaway
when the last three weeks are up.

I'd risk a diarrhea dump
by the side of I-5
to spend time on Earth
before they put me under the rays.
I'm thinking about where I'll stay.
I'm planning the rest of my days.

Home stretch.

I ring the bell to announce
I am through
with IVs, the long skinny tube,
and a bunch of medical personnel cheer.

The next day
I swallow the last steroid pill,
wait for the final Neulasta
On-Body Injector to fire.
I'll toss it in the Sharps Container
with the others,
ship it where medical waste goes.

The effects are cumulative.

It's harder to eat
food I could tolerate
during the last ten weeks.
Even water tastes bad.
Until my body expels
chemo-soaked shit,
I live in a chemical hum.
Four long days.

And the poison makes me tear
in ways I haven't faced before—
like this nosebleed
in a Del Mar Starbucks.
I thought I had congestion.

109 degrees
in the city of Santee means
the beach.
A breeze moves over teal waves,
cool, crisp—clean.

I've been drinking lots of water
to clear the toxins,
drain these chemicals.
The stairs are there.
Will they (did they)
alter the conditions
that bred this cancer?
Block my estrogen?
Find the right place to radiate?
I've been carved up,
chemically treated,
each subsequent step
a release.

Two lizards are back—
courting by the pool.
This time the male
darts past the female.
He stops in front of me
to perform a fine set of push-ups.

Flirting with wellness,
writing all morning—
getting chores done.
Light-headedness sends me back to bed.

Before radiation
can attack what's left,
the stylist takes her shears
to the last stragglers.
My hair can grow back evenly now.

The road trip
has been canceled
due to more nosebleeds.
They should go away as you recover.
I plan to fly instead.

Fireworks
in the backyard night.
Independence Day!

It is time to reassure this body—
no more poison.
I reassure it again.
A little better—
then a bit better.
No longer marinating
in chemicals—
I smell them though.
A meal out
and this bubble
defies the pull of Hades—
it lifts.
Yet a strange attachment
to the dungeon
persists.

ACT FOUR: Radiation

After discussing my case,
they add a step:
radiate lymph nodes
above and around my left clavicle,
on top of those
remaining near my armpit
(where they took two)
and the site where the tumor once lay
inside my breast.

The next prescription:

Time off!

I exist inside a post-chemo body.
It lacks a certain spark
that kindles to acupuncture needles,
though not completely.

I savor simple delights;
discard those too complex,
too rich, or too spicy.
Green scenes are a pleasure,
as are nature sounds—
gulls, crows, the sea,
the rain of summer storms.

UCSD Medical leaves a voicemail,
interrupting the happiness
I've almost found in Oregon.

Radiation Oncology.

How much cancer is left?
This question is my stalker.

The CT scan is not diagnostic,
a radiation therapist informs me,
before sending me on a ride
through the white circle.

They prick me with tattoos,
marks that are permanent.
Little black freckles.

Another breather
while they prepare;
but I'm anxious to know
the results
of the three trials.

Yoga breaks up the wait.
It is gentle, meditative,
and upset rises.
I tune into the tight spots,
the mass of feelings
vibrating in knotted muscles.
I still have aspirations
for this physical mechanism
pummeled by treatment.
Yet a different soreness burns
in places that call for peeling
layers into loving exhalation.
My life yearns to be sculpted
into lines that glisten.

For the next thirty business days,
I will commute
to Moores Cancer Center.
I just finished the dry run,
meant to help me practice—
help them get ready.

I will receive these treatments
on my back,
with my arms overhead,
chin slightly to the right.
They've placed a sticker on the wounded breast.
You'll have one there the whole six weeks.
They line the tattoos up,
so the newest technology
will keep most of the radiation
away from my heart.

I refuse the music
intended to take me from the rays.
I've decided to push
my Zen practice,
remaining still
beneath a machine
that looks like a giant faucet.
It hums as the spout-like appendage
arcs over me.
The circle at the end of this limb
contains a square lens.
Mysterious mechanisms move
behind this lens.
Something shoots a green light
in a long streak across the face of the circle.
Occasionally the circle turns.
I hear whirs, a knocking sound,
a click.
The circle moves away,
and then a square-like shape descends:
X-rays to confirm
everything is where it should be.

The real deal.
They use a self check-in system.
I scan my barcode

and head to the waiting area.
I hear a cough.
Without thinking, I become tense,
until I remember
my immune system is better.
They call my name,
lead me to the dressing room.
I put on a gown and sit down
in another waiting area
where I can see through a doorway
two sets of signs that light up:

Beam On

(this one lights up in red).

X-Ray On

(in black and white).

Generator On

(in black and white).

The Beam On signs are dark.
The X-Ray On signs are dark.
Both generator signs are on.
The X-Ray sign on the left lights up
before it goes dark.
It lights up again—
then it goes dark.
I am led to the room on the right.
It is called WINDANSEA.

They always take time
to position my body,
checking the markers on my uncovered breast,

sometimes measuring.
They tug at the sheet beneath me,
roll my gown back in places.
The big circle hovers above my chest.
Then they leave the room.
I know they can see me.
I know they can hear me.
I am not supposed to move.
What if I become a spaz?

During my first treatment,
the big circle moves a few times,
stopping to shoot some photons:
a thump followed by a whining
(occasionally there are whirring sounds).
At some point a rectangle descends,
then slides over me before popping up
to level out.
I think this instrument takes pictures.
During my second treatment,
only the circle is used.
During my fifth treatment,
they take more pictures.

On the weekend,
I wear sunscreen all day
on my neck and shoulders—
deodorant in my left pit.
During the week,
I leave these areas bare—
skin products will worsen the burns.

I want to support the healing process
with wise nutrition,
but so many good foods
contain antioxidants.
I need to *avoid* antioxidants.
Radiation kills by oxidation.

I finally get to the Y—
first time since pre-op.
I ride the stationary bike—
walk the treadmill—
feeling better than I have.

Second week—first zap.
I study the picture of the baby
with a clenched fist.
It is taped to the machine
for my entertainment.
Last week I didn't notice the words…

HEY
YOU CAN DO IT

Relief Lotion
becomes a daily ritual.
I massage it with care
into my left breast,
my left armpit,
around my left shoulder.
Not too pink just yet.

The weekend is something
to covet—
no treatment.
But I do get a sunburn
on my way to the Hollywood Bowl.
My doctor suggests it will heal
before the radiation burn sets in.
At least I enjoyed a full bowl:
Yo-Yo Ma and the Silk Road Ensemble.

Four more weeks—

A silent kinship exists
between patients
waiting.

I am making peace
with the space age thing
that comes right up to my face
for one treatment.
It hovers over-chest for another.
It also shoots from the left.
At times a red beam crosses my nose.

Strange to watch
some tissue becoming compromised,
feel fatigue,
while other parts of me heal.
My hair is growing in—
that alien sensibility
almost gone.

When they position me,
I can see the indistinct outline
of my uncovered breast
in the big lens—
also, a small white light.
They do pull up my hospital gown
before leaving the room.

Session fifteen:
they take more pictures,
making sure I'm still aligned;
replace the sticker on my breast.
Finally, I am zapped.

Half way!

A rash.
They prescribe a steroid cream
to prevent itching.

I count and recount—
cross out appointments.

Twelve left.

More pictures,
the usual zaps.

In preparation for the final boost,
they draw a map on a transparency,
place a sticker on the incision wound,
and dot little marks around this sticker.

Bull's eye.

Ten more treatments.

Angry rash.
Radiation burn,
some oozing
that could get infected.

Your breast may shrink—
like having a boob job.

I offset what's marred
by working with what I've got:
manicure
pedicure
leave the head cover off.

Boost
(last five treatments).
They check their map,
attach an extension to the big circle,
and aim it right
at the lumpectomy cavity.
My breast is exposed
when they shoot electrons
through this cone.

Radiation burns don't heal
the way sunburns do.

Second to last day.

I see my doctor
and she prescribes
silver sulfadiazine cream
for the three hot spots
that hurt when I try to sleep.

The final zap.
Now my body knows
how much radiation
it must recover from.

I get out of the cradle,
put my clothes on.
Radiation therapists
follow me to the lobby
for a quick ceremony.
They call it a graduation.
One therapist says a few lines—
then I ring the bell.
They give me a certificate.
Tears move in.
A friend takes photos.

I bid the therapists farewell.
We head to Seasons 52:
champagne and a good meal.
Afterwards,
a chick flick.

Tomorrow
is the first day of fall.
My plants have been drinking
unexpected rain.
No treatment today—
and no more treatments scheduled,
with the exception
of the daily pill I must take
for the next five years.

ACT FIVE: Follow-up

Throughout
the three trials,
I faced
what stayed with me:
scar across my left breast
missing lymph nodes
forced menopause
lack of stamina
stiff joints
rewired hair.

I am alive,
but am I free?

I see the radiation oncologist.
I ask her,
*What will happen
if it comes back?*

*Depends.
If it's in the left breast,
a mastectomy.
If it's somewhere else,
maybe radiation
or some other therapy.*

I see the surgeon.
I ask her,
*What will happen
if it comes back?*

We'll remove the breast.
But she hopes
the cancer is gone.

I see the medical oncologist.
I ask her,

*What will happen
if it comes back?*

*Depends.
If it's in the same breast,
surgery to remove it.
You could have chemo.
If it appears somewhere else,
other problems.
The brain,
that's the scariest—
vision loss,
headaches, seizures.
You should also watch for:
persistent pain (10-14 days)
unexplained weight loss
trouble breathing
strange coughing.
That said,
you've got to do everything you can do
and forget about it.*

The final therapy
(fingers crossed!)
is an aromatase inhibiter,
a daily pill prescribed
for post-menopausal women.
Since chemo switched my ovaries off,
they could rebel—wake up.
The doctor will monitor
hormone levels.
If I become fertile once more,
she'll shut me down
with a monthly shot.

It is said Persephone
climbed out of the land of the dead
to give us spring.
I've returned to autumn,
to Santa Ana winds;
to regular screens—
annual mammograms
to see where I am.
Soon I'll be eligible
for 55 and up housing,
some senior discounts.
Though in seven years,
all my atoms will be different—
and if no more spiders
move into my dreams,
restored.
For the moment,
a visceral nudge
prompts me
to do something new.

Kari Wergeland, who hails from Davis, California, is a librarian and writer. She moved to Oregon at the age of 14 and eventually attended the University of Oregon, where she earned a B.A. in English. She also holds an M.L.S. in Librarianship from the University of Washington and an M.F.A. in Creative Writing with an emphasis in poetry from Pacific University. Her work has appeared in many journals, including *Catamaran Literary Reader, Jabberwock Review: A Journal of Literature and Art, The Delmarva Review, New Millennium Writings, Pembroke Magazine, Broad Street, Wisconsin Review,* and *Crannóg*. She is the author of *Voice Break* and *The Ballad of the New Carissa and Other Poems*. Wergeland has just retired from a long career that took her into libraries up and down the West Coast. At some point in all of this, she served as a children's book reviewer for *The Seattle Times*.

CPSIA information can be obtained
at www.ICGtesting.com
Printed in the USA
BVHW03s0243030718
520697BV00001B/18/P

9 781635 345704